DISCARDED

D0918337

Cornerstones of Freedom

The Cuban Missile Crisis

Susan Maloney Clinton

CHILDRENS PRESS®
CHICAGO

MISSILE ERECTOR

CABLE

MISSILE SHELTER TENT

TRACKED PRIME MOVERS

FUEL TANK TRAILERS

Library of Congress Cataloging-in-Publication Data

Clinton, Susan.
  The Cuban missile crisis / by Susan Maloney Clinton.
    p. cm. — (Cornerstones of freedom)
  Summary: Presents the details of the 1962
confrontation between the United States and the Soviet
Union over the placement of Russian offensive missiles
in Cuba.
  ISBN 0-516-06667-6
  1. Cuban Missile Crisis, 1962—Juvenile literature.
[1. Cuban Missile Crisis, 1962.] I. Title. II. Series.
E841.C56 1993
327.73047'09'046—dc20   93-12689
[B]   CIP
                                            AC

The Cuban missile crisis began on October 15, 1962, with a set of black-and-white photographs. To an untrained eye, these photographs don't look like much. They look down, from a great height, on some kind of wilderness camp. One can make out tire tracks crisscrossing every which way through dark clumps of palm trees. A few things show up brightly against this dim landscape—some long shapes, a light splotch, a line of rectangles. When photo experts in Washington, D.C., saw these pictures, however, they knew exactly what they were looking at and they could hardly believe their eyes.

MISSILES

INITIAL IDENTIFICATION OF
MRBM MISSILES IN CUBA
MRBM LAUNCH SITE 1
SAN CRISTOBAL, CUBA

14 OCTOBER, 1962

Convoy

These top-secret photographs (left and opposite page), taken by U.S. spy planes, revealed Soviet nuclear missiles on Cuban soil.

With U-2 planes, the U.S. military could take surveillance photographs from as high as thirteen miles.

They had seen these very shapes, this arrangement of shapes, in photographs taken by U.S. military planes flying over the Soviet Union. Like the new photos, those of the Soviet Union had been shot by cameras mounted under a U-2. The U-2 was a jet plane with a wingspan longer than its body. It could zoom up thirteen miles and operate up there at 460 miles an hour. The United States used U-2s to gather information about the military forces of other countries. In short, the U-2s were spy planes. In the late 1950s, American U-2s flew regularly over the Soviet Union, taking thousands of pictures like these.

The long shapes in the new photos were truck trailers more than sixty feet long, built to carry missiles. The splotch was a patch of ground recently dug up to build a launching pad. The line of rectangles was a line of tank trucks carrying missile fuel. The photo experts were looking at pictures of a Soviet nuclear missile base. But this base was not being built in the Soviet Union, half a world away. It was in Cuba, an island nation only about ninety miles away from Florida. From this Cuban base, the missiles would be able to strike Miami, New Orleans, Atlanta, or Washington, D.C.

President John F. Kennedy

The next morning, in Washington, American president John F. Kennedy was sitting on the edge of his bed skimming the morning papers when the report on the Cuban missile bases came

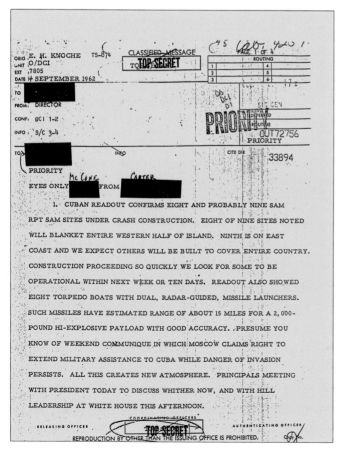

These top-secret CIA memos confirm the sighting of missiles in Cuba (left) and show the potential range of missiles launched from Cuba (below).

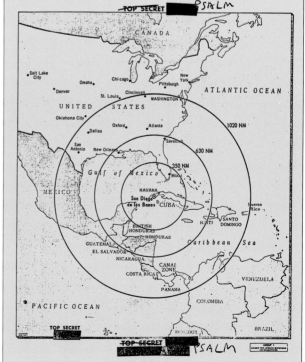

in. As Kennedy looked at the photos, he was startled, then angry. Roughly a month before, he had issued a warning to Nikita Khrushchev, the leader of the Soviet Union, about sending offensive weapons to Cuba. He now realized that this warning had come too late.

Cuba had been a grating irritation to American leaders ever since revolutionary leader Fidel Castro had taken over in January 1959. Castro was not friendly to the United States and made this clear in public speeches that lasted for hours. His government took over plantations and factories in the name of the Cuban people without paying American owners anything for them. The United States cut off trade with Cuba. Castro turned to the Soviet Union.

Cuban prime minister Fidel Castro

Castro greets his ally, Soviet premier Nikita Khrushchev, at a United Nations meeting. The Soviets' close ties to Cuba aroused American fears of a communist invasion of the West.

The sight of Fidel Castro and Soviet leader Nikita Khrushchev embracing at a United Nations meeting made American politicians and military leaders very unhappy. They feared that the Soviets would use Cuba as a jumping-off point for spreading Communism, revolution, and weapons throughout Latin America. In 1960, President Kennedy even backed an invasion of Cuba by a force of Cuban exiles. Their goal was to overthrow Castro. They landed at the Bay of Pigs and were quickly overrun by Castro's troops.

Khrushchev lashes out at the United States during a 1960 speech.

The invasion was a disastrous failure. It made Kennedy look foolish and indecisive. It convinced Castro that he needed protection. And it gave Nikita Khrushchev an excuse for planting nuclear missiles in Cuba.

Nikita Khrushchev had headed the Soviet Union for seven years. He was a forceful personality and a shrewd political fighter. He had risen from a youth of poverty and survived treacherous political struggles to become the leader of a world superpower. Americans remembered the bald and burly Khrushchev pounding his shoe on a table to emphasize a point in the United Nations. He could not have been more unlike his American counterpart.

John F. Kennedy was the youngest man ever elected to the American presidency. Born of a wealthy and powerful family, Kennedy had a quick wit and polished manner. He brought an athletic vigor to the White House. During his presidential campaign, Kennedy had promised to stand firm against the Soviets; now his resolve would be tested against Nikita Khrushchev's in a dangerous Cold War confrontation—the leader of the Free World against the leader of the Communist World.

Since 1945, the U.S. and the Soviet Union had been locked in a bitter struggle for world

Kennedy's campaign promise to stand up to the Soviets was soon put to the test.

leadership. Their governments were based on different principles; each one believed that the world would be better off following its system. Soon Europe was divided into two camps— Western Europe allied itself with the democratic United States, and Eastern Europe was dominated by the communist Soviet Union.

As other countries went through revolutions, both the United States and the Soviet Union would jump into the struggle. Rival groups supported by the rival superpowers would fight one another for control in these emerging nations. With every superpower confrontation, the threat of a nuclear war hung over the world.

During this period, the Soviet Union and the United States were the only nations that had nuclear weapons. Both sides knew what terrible damage these weapons could do. One nuclear bomb could destroy an entire city, kill millions of people, and poison the air, land, and water for ages to come. Neither side actually wanted to use these awful weapons. Both sides hoped that the fear of a nuclear strike would be enough to prevent, or deter, the other from ever launching an attack. Nonetheless, both sides raced to build more and powerful weapons. Each side tried to hide its advances and uncover the other's. This superpower conflict was called the Cold War, because it was a war of fear and threats and secrets rather than one of actual battles.

As Kennedy looked at the photos, he knew that the United States had just discovered a dangerous Cold War secret. He also knew how important it was to conceal the information while he decided what to do. If news of nuclear missile bases so close to the United States leaked out to the public, it would cause a widespread panic and a pressing clamor for war. Kennedy knew he had to do something, but he did not want his choice to be forced upon him. He also wanted to surprise the Soviets. Let them go on thinking their missiles were a secret just a little while longer.

Kennedy called for a meeting and listed the men he wanted there—his brother, Attorney General Robert Kennedy; Secretary of State Dean Rusk and Defense Secretary Robert McNamara;

President Kennedy (right) confers with his brother, Attorney General Robert F. Kennedy.

The president with Secretary of Defense Robert McNamara

several military men; an expert on Latin America; an expert on the Soviet leadership; and several other high-level advisors—all men whose knowledge, judgment, and loyalty he valued. This informal group came to be called EXCOM, the Executive Committee of the National Security Council. Throughout the crisis, President Kennedy would rely on their advice.

At this first meeting, everyone agreed on one thing: the United States simply could not allow this threat so close to home. Their goal was to get the missiles out. The question was, how?

At first, most of them believed that a surprise air strike would be the best and the fastest way to end the threat. Kennedy was angry and wanted action. But as the EXCOM members figured out exactly what it would take, some of them began to change their minds. An air attack would not be that fast or that simple. The Soviets had also given Cuba antiaircraft guns and fighter planes. Any bombing attack would have to begin by destroying the Cuban radar system, then the antiaircraft guns. The next targets would be fighter planes; only then could American bombers go in to knock out the missiles. Even then, the Air Force couldn't guarantee that the nuclear missiles would be 100 percent destroyed.

Some EXCOM members were worried— wouldn't all this bombing kill lots of people, Cubans and Soviets alike? Wouldn't the Soviet

A meeting of EXCOM during the Cuban missile crisis

Union have to take some action if many Soviets and Cubans were killed? Perhaps the Soviets would strike at U.S. missiles in Turkey, close to the Soviet border. Then how would the United States respond?

President Kennedy met with Adlai Stevenson, the U.S. delegate to the United Nations. Stevenson was against starting with any kind of an attack. He suggested that Kennedy try negotiating first, but Kennedy and EXCOM roundly rejected this suggestion. They wanted action, not talk. Talking first would just give the Soviets more time to finish building the bases.

President Kennedy meets with Adlai Stevenson, the American ambassador to the United Nations (with hat); Stevenson advised against military action at the beginning of the crisis.

Sometime that evening, EXCOM came up with the idea of a naval quarantine. U.S. ships could surround the island and turn back any ships carrying military cargo. A quarantine would keep weapons from coming in without killing anyone. It would get the world's attention without drawing the world's anger. Some argued against it. How would a blockade get the missiles out? The United States could blockade Cuba for months without budging one missile.

For the next four days, EXCOM was split into "hawks," who favored an attack, and "doves," who wanted to try the quarantine first. The hawks didn't believe the Soviets would use their nuclear weapons, even if the United States attacked. After all, they argued, exactly how great was the danger from these Cuban missiles?

Surprisingly, everyone agreed that even with the existence of the Cuban missiles, the United States was still way ahead of the Soviet Union in nuclear weapons. True, these missiles could reach targets out of reach to the Soviets before. But the United States still had more missiles and more accurate missiles. It had missiles close to the Soviet Union, in Turkey, and missiles that could be launched from submarines cruising Mediterranean or Pacific waters. The Soviet Union could not hope to win a nuclear war against the United States. Secretary of the Treasury Douglas Dillon, an EXCOM member, later explained, "You could not help thinking about those missiles pointed at us just a few miles off the Florida coast. But, at the same time, I never thought the Soviets would use the missiles. I mean, if they had, they would have been committing suicide, and I never thought they'd do that."

The doves weren't so sure. They thought about the man who controlled the bombs. What if Nikita Khrushchev decided to teach his arrogant enemy a lesson, to show his toughness to the world? What if he fired even one missile? Secretary of State Dean Rusk later said, "I think we always have to leave open the unpredictability

Secretary of the Treasury Douglas Dillon

Secretary of State Dean Rusk

Top military officials leave an emergency meeting at the White House as the president prepares to announce the quarantine.

of what an actual living, breathing human being would do in a situation. . . . Those who really understand nuclear weapons understand that nuclear war is simply that war which must not be fought, because it not only eliminates all the answers, it eliminates all the questions."

Time was growing short. News reporters were beginning to wonder about all the comings and goings at the White House. The president pressed for a decision. EXCOM chose the quarantine. True, it would not directly force the missiles out, but it would be a strong gesture. It was more than words and less than war.

Kennedy agreed; he would start with a quarantine. Now, it was time to tell the world. On

Monday, October 22, specially chosen ambassadors flew to Canada, Great Britain, France, and Germany to inform Allied governments. The three major television networks cleared their 7:00 P.M. time slot for the president's message to the nation. Early that evening, Kennedy briefed a group of influential American congressmen. Kennedy had to argue with those who wanted to invade Cuba and overthrow Castro once and for all. He said, "Last Tuesday, I was for an air strike or an invasion myself, but after four more days of deliberations, we decided that was not the wisest first move, and you would, too, if you had more time to think about it."

Kennedy's decision to surround Cuba with a naval blockade (left) became the subject of a number of political cartoons (right).

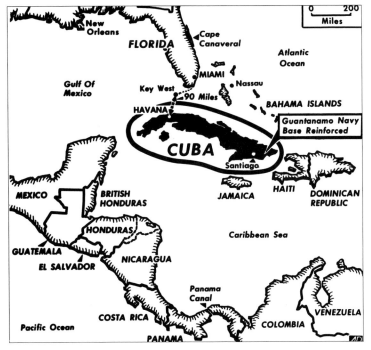

"I'd Reconsider If I Were You!"

October 22, 1962: Kennedy announces the crisis to the world.

Meanwhile, Secretary of State Rusk sat down with Soviet Ambassador Anatoly Dobrynin. Dobrynin walked into the White House smiling and left pale and haggard. He had read a copy of the speech the president was about to make. At the same time, Nikita Khrushchev was receiving a copy of the speech in Moscow.

At 6:59 that Monday night, the president entered the Oval Office. The room was crowded with TV cameras, lights, and microphones ready to broadcast his speech to the American people. Kennedy spoke for seventeen minutes. In a calm, even voice, he told the nation about the missile bases and announced what steps he was taking—a naval quarantine, a military alert for American forces, continued U-2 flights over Cuba, a call for a UN meeting.

Kennedy remained calm and assured as he announced his plan.

Kennedy did all he could in his speech to downplay feelings of fear and anger. He looked calm and sure of himself; his voice was even and unemotional. He was not trying to rouse the American people to war. He was coaching an entire nation in how to live through a Cold War confrontation with patience and self-restraint. He closed by urging the American people to be prepared for a time "in which both our will and our patience will be tested."

People gather in a hotel lobby to watch Kennedy's televised speech.

Kennedy signs the quarantine proclamation.

After Kennedy's speech, some Americans rallied for war, while others marched in demonstrations for peace. Many charged into supermarkets and bought wildly, stocking up food in case of a nuclear disaster. Most simply waited, watched, and worried. That night, as Americans went to bed, many wondered if they would wake up the next day. The next morning, Dean Rusk found his assistant secretary asleep on a couch in his office. He woke him up saying, "We have won a considerable victory. You and I are still alive." There was a feeling of relief; the crisis wasn't over, but it was out in the open and nothing terrible had happened yet.

Some people rallied in support of the president's decision (right), while others protested against it (left).

The day after Kennedy's announcement, U.S. military forces mobilize for the quarantine and also prepare for the worst—an all-out invasion of Cuba.

That day, American forces all over the world were put at a new stage of alert. American bombers, which routinely flew with their bomb bays open to show that they had no weapons, now flew with the bays loaded and shut. An army of 200,000 men was massed in Florida, ready in case President Kennedy ordered an invasion. American cruisers and destroyers moved to block the five main sea channels into Cuba. American naval destroyers searched the seas to locate Russian ships and submarines. They found twenty-three Soviet ships sailing towards Cuba,

October 25: The U.S. spy photos are revealed at a tense UN meeting.

three of them big enough to be carrying missiles.

Kennedy received a letter from Khrushchev. The Soviet leader was furious. He claimed that all the weapons in Cuba were there for the island's defense. The quarantine was an unjustified act of aggression, "a serious threat to peace and security of peoples." Khrushchev was not going to back down an inch.

The quarantine began officially at 10:00 A.M. on Wednesday, October 24, 1962. Two Soviet ships were due to reach the quarantine line at about 10:15. Kennedy and his advisors waited tensely. Would the Soviet ships try to sail through? Everyone felt that war could be minutes away.

Finally, the report came in. All twenty-three Russian ships were stopping. Sixteen of them had turned around and were sailing back to port. The quarantine would not be tested that day. Dean Rusk remarked, "We're eyeball to eyeball and I think the other fellow just blinked."

On Thursday, October 25, Adlai Stevenson confronted Soviet delegate Valerian Zorin at a United Nations meeting. "Do you, Ambassador Zorin, deny that the U.S.S.R. has placed and is placing medium- and intermediate-range missiles and sites in Cuba? Yes or no—don't wait for the translation—yes or no." Zorin refused to commit himself, saying, "In due course, sir, you will have your reply." Stevenson sent a ripple of laughter through the assembly when he answered, "I am prepared to wait for my answer until hell freezes

The drama thickens in the UN as Stevenson (right) challenges Zorin (left) to deny the existence of Soviet missiles in Cuba.

over, if that is your decision." Stevenson finished by saying, "Our job here is not to score debating points. Our job, Mr. Zorin, is to save the peace. And if you are ready to try, we are."

Meanwhile, Khrushchev did not seem ready to try. He had ordered the Soviet ships to resume sailing toward Cuba. The first one to approach the quarantine line was a tanker called the *Bucharest*. The Americans already knew that it carried only oil. Kennedy ordered the quarantine commanders to question the *Bucharest* by radio, but not to try to stop or board it. The president did not want to use force against a ship that he knew was no threat.

He also did not want to rush Khrushchev. Kennedy had been thinking about this crisis for more than a week; his anger and outrage had cooled. But Khrushchev had only had three days and Kennedy knew that the Soviet leader was in no mood for compromise. The Soviet tanker was allowed to pass. It was the first Soviet-American contact on the quarantine line.

Early on Friday, October 26, two American warships stopped a ship called the *Marcula* at the quarantine line. Kennedy had singled out the *Marcula* not because it was suspicious, but because it was a safe target. Although it was carrying Soviet goods to Cuba, it was not a Soviet ship, nor was it carrying any military cargo. American officers boarded the smaller ship and

A U.S. officer returns to his ship after inspecting the Marcula.

A U.S. destroyer (foreground) moves alongside a Cuba-bound Russian freighter to inspect its cargo.

peered below decks at the heaps of cargo. After the inspection, the *Marcula* was allowed to sail on. Kennedy wanted to show his determination to enforce the quarantine without provoking any Soviet retaliation.

Later that day, the president received word that all Russian ships, except oil tankers, had turned back. The quarantine was working—no new military supplies could come into Cuba. But the missile bases remained. In fact, U-2 photos showed two alarming things. The Soviets were working faster—they were now digging and building through the night. And they were camouflaging the missiles to conceal them from the U-2s' cameras.

That night, there was a breakthrough. A long letter came to Kennedy from Khrushchev. The angry tone was gone. Khrushchev seemed to be feeling the weight of responsibility that only these two men had to bear. He wrote, "We and you ought not now to pull on the ends of the rope in which you have tied the knot of war, because the more the two of us pull, the tighter that knot will be tied, and a moment may come when that knot will be tied so tight that even he who tied it will not have strength to untie it, and then it will be necessary to cut that knot. . . . Let us not only relax the forces pulling on the ends of the rope; let us take measures to untie that knot. We are ready for this."

If the United States would promise not to invade Cuba, Khrushchev suggested, the Soviets would remove the missiles. American hopes for a peaceful solution soared, only to be crushed the very next day by two new events. First came a new letter from Khrushchev. He was changing his offer, adding new demands. Now Khrushchev was insisting on an open trade—he would take out the Cuban missiles only if the U.S. would take its missiles out of Turkey. Kennedy and

EXCOM began to wonder if the Soviets were trying to trick them. Maybe Khrushchev was stalling for time to finish the missile bases. Kennedy felt he could not back down on this. The United States would not trade missile for missile; the Cuban missiles simply had to go.

Worse yet, that morning, an American U-2 flying over Cuba was hit by a Soviet SAM, a surface-to-air missile. The plane crashed into the jungle; its pilot was killed instantly. Four days before, Kennedy and EXCOM had decided that if an American plane were hit, the U.S. would instantly strike back by bombing a Soviet SAM installation. The hawks on EXCOM urged an air strike, followed by an invasion. Air force bombers were preparing for flight at that moment.

Kennedy made a decision; he called off the bombers. Maybe, maybe the shoot-down had been a mistake. He wanted to try one last time to avoid war. It was Robert Kennedy who came up with a way to make this last peace offer. He suggested that Kennedy ignore the demands in Khrushchev's second letter and accept the offer in the first letter. Kennedy approved. His acceptance letter went to Khrushchev in Moscow while Bobby Kennedy went to see Ambassador Dobrynin. Bobby put his case as forcefully as he could. If the Soviets did not accept this last offer within one day, the president could no longer hold back the hawks. War was one day away.

Major Rudolf Anderson, the pilot of the U-2 shot down by a Soviet SAM during the crisis

Reporters are told that the crisis is over.

Finally, on Sunday, October 28, at nine in the morning, Khrushchev broadcast a message over Moscow radio: "The Soviet government . . . has given a new order to dismantle the weapons, which you describe as offensive, and to crate them and return them to the Soviet Union." The missile crisis was over. There was a tremendous feeling of relief and joy. As one official recalled, "All of a sudden this huge burden was lifted and I felt like laughing or yelling or dancing. . . . It was a marvelous morning. I'll never forget it as long as I live."

November 2: An aerial photograph shows Soviet missiles being loaded for transport out of Cuba.

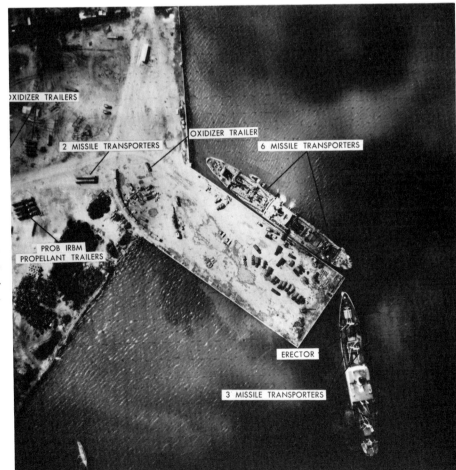

A Soviet freighter leaves Cuba with a cargo of tarp-covered missiles.

The one who was angry was Castro.

He didn't trust the Americans or their promises and he refused to follow the agreement. Although the agreement called for the UN to witness the dismantling of the bases, Castro would not allow any observers. The U.S. had to settle for U-2 flights to keep track of the missiles. Soviet ship captains rolled back the heavy tarps covering the missile crates so that U-2s could snap photos. Passes over the former missile bases showed only mounds of dirt and empty roads. On November 21, 1962, President Kennedy lifted the quarantine. The crisis was over, but things would never be just as they had been before.

After the crisis was over, Kennedy and Khrushchev met amicably and agreed to a nuclear test ban treaty.

Kennedy and Khrushchev had found a peaceful way out of the confrontation in spite of mistrust, distance, and pressure from their own countrymen to take an unyielding stand. With the downing of the American U-2, both leaders realized how easy it would be to slip into war by accident. That experience of coming close to nuclear war gave both leaders a new respect for one another. As Khrushchev had said in his letter, they were connected like two men holding the two ends of a rope.

After the Cuban missile crisis, Kennedy and Khrushchev were able to agree to a nuclear test ban treaty—neither superpower would explode any nuclear bombs in the earth's atmosphere. They installed a hot line—a phone connection from Washington to Moscow so that the two leaders could talk directly instead of relying on radio broadcasts or cable messages. Neither leader ever claimed the missile crisis as a victory. But Khrushchev got the last word. When Kennedy was assassinated, a little over a year later, in November 1963, Khrushchev said about him, "He was gifted with the ability to resolve international conflicts by negotiation, as the whole world learned during the so-called Cuban crisis. . . . He showed great flexibility and, together, we avoided disaster."

President Kennedy signs the Nuclear Test Ban Treaty.

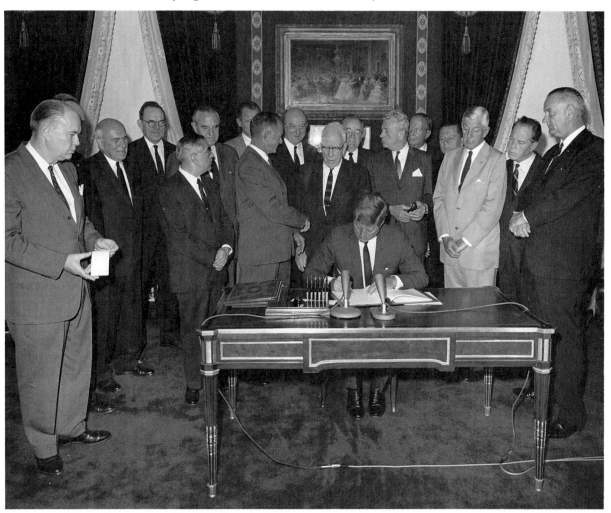

INDEX

PHOTO CREDITS

Cover, UPI/Bettmann; 1, AP/Wide World; 2, UPI/Bettmann; 3, CIA; 4, Department of the Air Force; 5 (top),
John F. Kennedy Library; 5 (bottom), approved for release through the Historical Review Program of the
Central Intelligence Agency, 10 September 1992, HRP 92-9; 6, 7, AP/Wide World; 8, UPI/Bettmann; 9, 10,
11 (top), AP/Wide World; 11 (bottom), John F. Kennedy Library; 13, 14, 15, 16, UPI/Bettmann; 17 (left),
AP/Wide World; 17 (right), Richard Q. Yardley, *The Baltimore Sun*, permission of Susan Yardley Wheltle;
18, 19 (bottom), AP/Wide World; 19 (top), John F. Kennedy Library; 20 (top), UPI/Bettmann; 20 (bottom),
AP/Wide World; 21, 22, 23, UPI/Bettmann; 24, Official U.S. Navy Photograph; 25, 27, 28 (bottom),
AP/Wide World; 28 (top), 29, UPI/Bettmann; 30, 31, John F. Kennedy Library

Picture Identifications:
Cover: Cuban refugees in New York City watch President Kennedy's
televised address on October 22, 1962.
Page 1: President Kennedy deep in thought in the Oval Office

Project Editor: Shari Joffe
Designer: Karen Yops
Photo Research: Jan Izzo
Cornerstones of Freedom Logo: David Cunningham

ABOUT THE AUTHOR

Susan Maloney Clinton holds a Ph.D. in English and is a part-time teacher of English literature at
Northwestern University. Her articles have appeared in such publications as *Consumer's Digest, Family
Style Magazine,* and the Chicago *Reader.* In addition, she has contributed biographical and historical
articles to *Encyclopaedia Britannica* and *Compton's Encyclopedia,* and has written reader stories and other
materials for a number of educational publishers. Ms. Clinton lives in Chicago with her husband, Pat, and
their three children.